ROPE &
RING
TRICKS

BRUCE SMITH

ARCTURUS

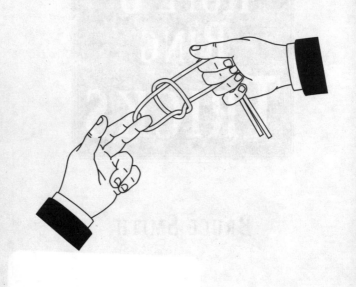

GLOSSARY OF TERMS

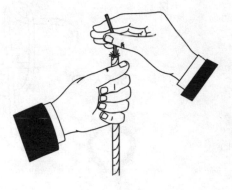

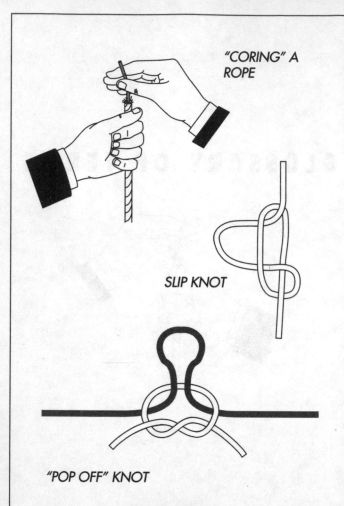

"CORING" A ROPE

SLIP KNOT

"POP OFF" KNOT

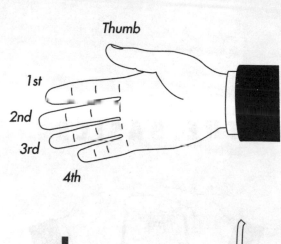

Thumb

1st

2nd

3rd

4th

SLIDING KNOT

OVERHAND KNOT

THE BASICS

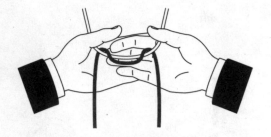

Effect *The magician ties a knot in the end of a length of rope using only one hand.*

Requirements *A length of rope about 75cm/30in long.*

Preparation *At one end of the rope tie an overhand knot (see Glossary) and conceal it in your right hand.*

• • • • • • • • • • • • • • •

1 Dangle the rope from your right hand, keeping the knot concealed inside your hand. We will refer to the knotted end of the rope as end A and the unknotted end as end B (see illustration 1).

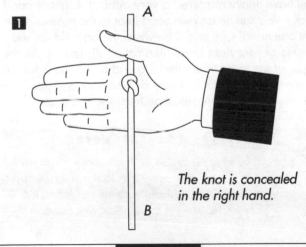

The knot is concealed in the right hand.

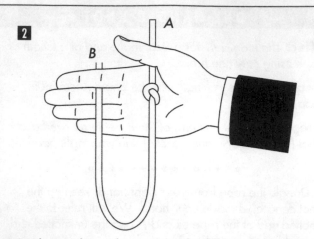

2 Explain to the audience that after hours of practice you have finally mastered a very difficult sleight-of-hand trick – you can tie an overhand knot in the rope using just one hand! Clip end B between the first and second fingers of your right hand (illustration 2). Then shake the rope, at the same time releasing end B. You have failed! You explain that this is a very difficult trick and you require absolute concentration from the audience.

TOP TIPS FOR TRICKSTERS

The best type of rope to use in these tricks is soft white cotton rope. There are many tips that will make this rope even easier to handle – check out the ROPE PREPARATION TIPS throughout this book.

---

3 Offer to attempt to do it again. Once again, bring end B up to your right hand and clip it between your fingers. Shake the rope, but this time hold on to end B and release end A (illustration 3). It seems you have magically tied an overhand knot in the end of the rope with just one hand. All those hours of practice paid off!

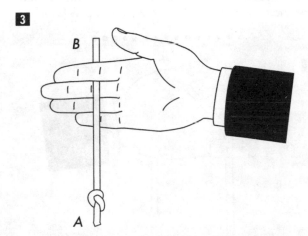

Effect *The magician ties a knot in a rope using only one hand.*

Requirements *A piece of rope about 65cm/25in long.*

Preparation *There is no preparation for this version of the trick – you really do tie a knot with one hand.*

• • • • • • • • • • • • • • • • •

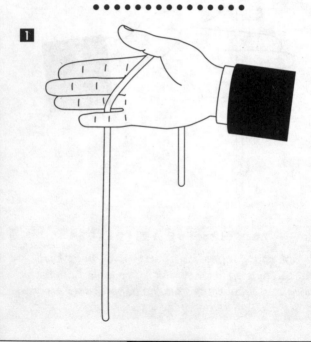

2

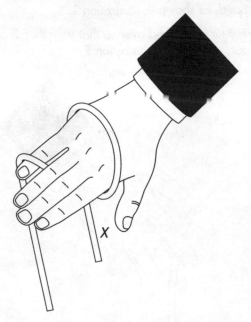

1 Drape the rope over your right hand as shown in illustration 1. The end hanging at the back should be slightly shorter than the end hanging at the front.

ROPE PREPARATION TIP

To make your rope even more flexible you can remove the inner core. This is known as "coring" a rope.

2 Clip the rope between the little and third fingers of the right hand, as shown in illustration 1.

3 Turn your right hand over so that your thumb points to the floor, as shown in illustration 2.

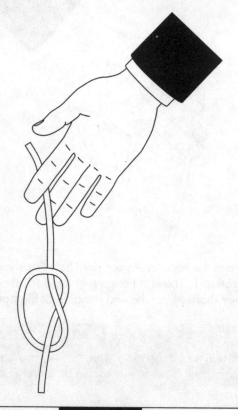

4 As your hand twists, your first and second fingers bend inwards and catch hold of the rope at the back just below the hand (at X on illustration 2). Give the rope a shake so that it falls off your hand. The piece of rope held by the first and second fingers will be pulled through the loop to form a knot (illustration 3).

5 As the rope falls, grab the other end with your left hand and pull it tight.

6 A knot will appear in the middle of the rope – as if by magic (illustration 4).

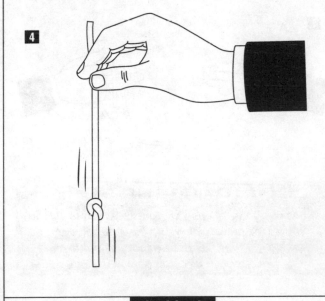

Effect *A knot mysteriously appears in the centre of a length of rope.*

Requirements *A rope about 75cm/30in long.*

Preparation *No preparation is required.*

• • • • • • • • • • • • • • • •

1 Hold end A of the rope in the left hand with the end pointing up. Drape end B over the back of the right hand so that end B rests in the right palm (illustration 1).

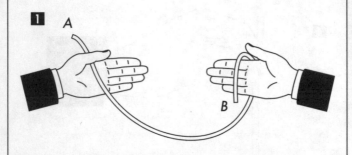

TOP TIPS FOR TRICKSTERS

When using newspaper for your tricks, remember to rub over the newsprint with a tissue to remove any excess ink. This will ensure that you finish your performance as clean as you started!

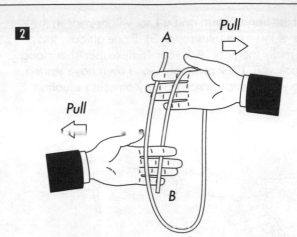

2 Move your hands towards each other. The righthand
first and second fingers clip end A above the left hand.
At the same time the lefthand first and second fingers
clip end B (illustration 2). As your hands move together
ask a spectator to time you with their watch to see how
long it takes you to tie a knot in the centre of the rope.
You can explain that it takes most people about ten
seconds.

ROPE PREPARATION TIP

*To "core" a length of rope, open the threads at one
end, grasp the inner core and slide off the outer shell
by pulling on the core and bunching up the shell.*

3 Pull the hands apart and a knot will appear in the centre of the rope (illustration 3). Done quickly, this looks really magical. Ask your "timekeeper" how long that took you. They probably won't even have started timing you – which creates a very amusing situation.

3

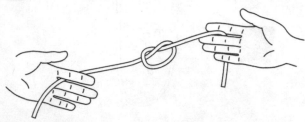

HARRY HOUDINI (1874-1926)

Houdini was famed all over the world for his daring and dangerous escapes from packing cases, handcuffs, straitjackets – and rope. Although some of the escapes described in this book may seem simple, a number of the methods were used by Houdini to help make him into the legend he is today. He died after a student punched him in the stomach to see if he was as powerful as he claimed. His death, on 31 October (Halloween) 1926, was ironic, as he had spent the years since the death of his beloved mother investigating and debunking spirit mediums.

Effect *A knot dissolves when it is pulled.*

Requirements *A length of rope at least 60cm/2ft.*

• • • • • • • • • • • • • • • • •

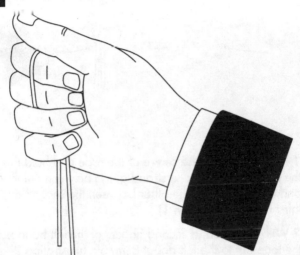

ROPE PREPARATION TIP

It is a good idea to "fix" the ends of any pieces of rope you may be using in your performance as this will prevent them from fraying.

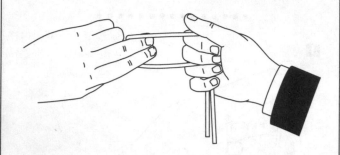

1 Make a loop at the centre of the rope and hold this in the right hand with one strand going between the thumb and first finger and the other between the second and third finger (illustration 1).

2 With the first and second fingers of the left hand pull the loop out to the left about 8cm/3in (illustration 2).

ROPE PREPARATION TIP

One way to "fix" the ends of a length of rope to stop them fraying is to dip them in white glue (for example, Copydex) and allow them to dry overnight.

3

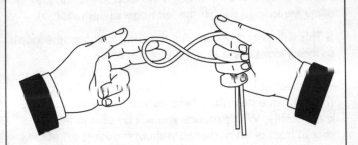

3 Twist the left hand to put a single twist in the loop (illustration 3).

4

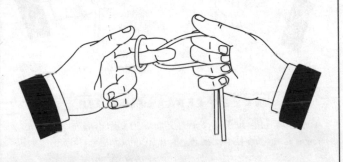

4 Slide the left first and second fingers through the loop and clip hold of the upper strand of rope (illustration 4). Pull the clipped strand through the loop to the left, and allow the loop to slip off the left fingers (illustration 5).

5 This will form a noose. Pull the ends to tighten the loop so that it looks like a knot (illustration 6).

This special knot can be used in many different tricks. The technique described teaches you how to prepare the knot secretly. With practice you will be able to tie this knot in front of an audience without arousing suspicion.

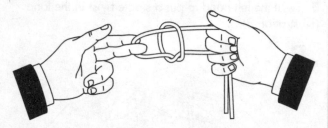

ROPE PREPARATION TIP

Another alternative for "fixing" the ends of a piece of rope is to dip them in molten wax. Unlike glue this will dry and harden in a few minutes.

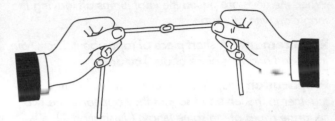

*When the ends are pulled hard,
the knot will disappear.*

THE INDIAN ROPE TRICK

*In reports of this effect an Indian street magician (fakir)
throws a long coil of rope into the air where it remains
vertically rigid. A boy climbs to the top and promptly
vanishes. The magician follows the boy to the top of
the rope carrying a large knife and vanishes as well.
The boy's severed limbs fall from the sky and are
collected in a basket by the magician upon his return.
Finally, the boy emerges unharmed from the basket. So
few people can lay claim to having seen this trick
performed that it is generally considered to be a myth.
Various magicians have managed to replicate the
effect on stage, but as yet no one has performed the
trick successfully in the open air.*

Effect *The magician ties two ropes together with a knot. When the ends are pulled the knot jumps off leaving the magician with one rope.*

Requirements *A short piece of rope about 15cm/6in long, and a longer piece about 1m/3ft.*

Preparation *Loop the two ropes and hold them together in the left hand so that they appear to be two separate ropes of the same length (illustration 1).*

• • • • • • • • • • • • • • •

1

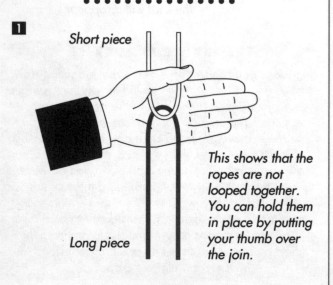

Short piece

Long piece

This shows that the ropes are not looped together. You can hold them in place by putting your thumb over the join.

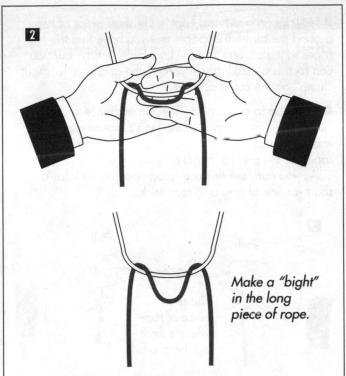

2

Make a "bight" in the long piece of rope.

1 Display the rope as two pieces of rope of equal length (illustration 1). Explain that neither rope is long enough so you are going to tie them together.

2 The right first finger pushes the centre of the long piece through the loop of the short piece (illustration 2). This forms a loop or "bight" in the long rope.

3 Now tie an overhand knot in the short piece of rope around the bight. It appears that you have tied the two ropes together. Say that the knot looks untidy, but you can fix this by asking everyone in the audience to shout "jump" on the count of three.

4 Count up to three, and when the audience shouts "jump" pull on the ends of the long piece of rope. The knot will jump off (illustration 3) and the long piece of rope will the perfect length for your next trick!

As you can, see this is a good opening trick for a short routine of ring and rope tricks.

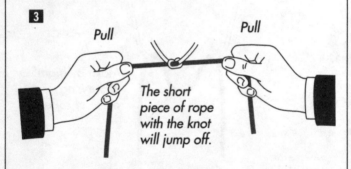

3

Pull

Pull

The short piece of rope with the knot will jump off.

ROPE PREPARATION TIP

You can sew the ends of the rope to "fix" them and prevent them fraying, or simply wrap the ends in white cotton to stop them unravelling.

Effect The magician knots together two ropes of equal length. The magician then slides the knot down to the bottom of one piece of the rope and unties it – to show one short rope and one long rope.

Requirements A short piece of rope (20cm/8in long) and a long rope (about 1m/3ft).

Preparation Loop the short piece of rope around the centre of the long piece (illustration 1).

• • • • • • • • • • • • • • • •

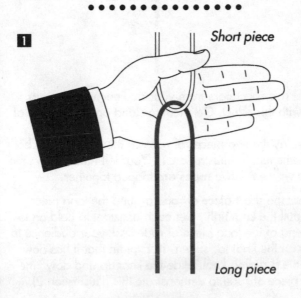

1

Short piece

Long piece

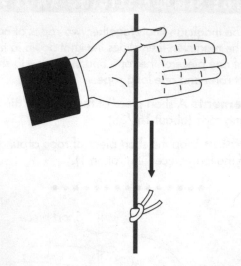

1 Get two spectators from your audience up to assist you with this effect. Get them to stand one either side of you.

Display the two pieces of rope as though they are both the same length (illustration 1). Your left hand covers the point where the two ropes are looped together.

2 Knot the short piece of rope around the long piece, and pull the knot tight. Get each assistant to hold on to one end of the long piece of rope. Ask your audience to blow on the knot to "soften" it. Explain that it has now become a sliding knot. Slide the knot up and down the long piece of rope to demonstrate this (illustration 2).

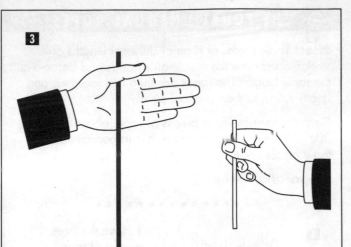

3 Slide the knot down the rope to about 10cm/4in from the end (illustration 2). Ask the person holding that end of the rope to let go, so that you can untie the knot.

4 Hold the knotted portion in your left hand and untie the knot with your right.

5 Separate the ropes to show one is now four times longer than the other (illustration 3). The ropes can be examined and kept by your two volunteers as souvenirs.

Effect Three pieces of rope of different lengths are stretched between the magician's hands and become all the same length! The ropes are then tied together, and finally return to their original sizes.

Requirements Three pieces of rope, about 60cm/2ft, 30cm/1ft and 20cm/8in long. It is important that all three pieces are the same colour.

Preparation None.

• • • • • • • • • • • • • • • • •

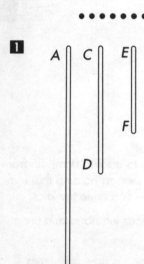

1 Have the three lengths of rope examined by the audience. Ask them to make sure the ropes do not stretch. Collect the ropes together.

2 You must clip one end of each rope between the left thumb and first finger. The order of the ropes must be as in illustration 1, so that the longest rope (AB) is nearest the thumb crotch.

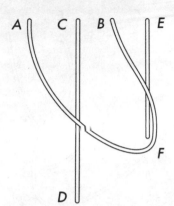

3 With your right hand bring end B up to the left first finger and thumb, so that it it clipped between ends C and E. Make sure that the rope passes over the top of rope EF as in illustration 2.

4 Now with your right hand bring up ends F and D into the left hand, placing them to the right of the other ends being clipped (illustration 3). You will see from the illustration that this procedure loops ropes AB and EF together. This prepares you for the "big stretch"!

5 Take ends A, C and B in your left hand and E, F and D in your right hand and slowly pull your hands apart. Amazingly it will appear that all three ropes stretch between your hands to become the same length (illustration 4). Keep your right hand closed around the point where the short and long ropes are linked.

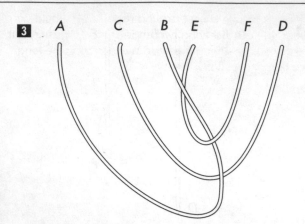

3 A   C   B E   F   D

6 To convince the audience that the three ropes really are of the same length you now perform a special false count. You appear to count the ropes singly from hand to hand – concealing the fact that two of them are looped together. Here's what really happens . . .
The right hand takes rope CD from the left hand as you say "one". The right hand then appears to take one of the two ropes in the left hand. It cannot do this as they are connected! So it swaps the single rope for the looped ropes. It does this by putting rope CD back into the left hand (clipped in the thumb crotch), and grasps the looped ropes with the right second and third fingers. Your right hand moves to the right as you say "two". The left hand then passes rope CD to the right hand again as you say "three".

7 Tie ends EF into a knot around rope AB. It should appear you are just tying two ends of rope together, but in reality you are tying the short piece around the long piece to make a sliding knot.

8 When the knot is tight and is not going to slip off the rope, let go and tie end B to end C. It should appear you are making a long length of all three ropes. Explain that even though the ropes are securely tied together you can still make them return to their original lengths.

9 Wrap the ropes around your left hand, but as you do so, slide the knot at the same time. Secretly move the knot until it is about 15cm/6in from one end of the long rope it is tied around.

10 Show the ropes coiled around your hand. Then snap your fingers – and uncoil the ropes to show they have now returned to their original length. It appears that you now have a short piece, tied to a long piece, tied to a medium-length piece of rope. All three ropes can be untied and examined by the audience.

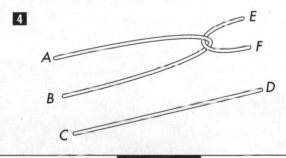

RINGS AND ROPE

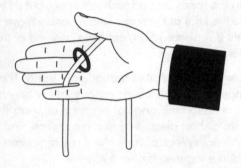

Effect *A bangle mysteriously penetrates on to a rope tied around both the magician's wrists.*

Requirements *A piece of rope about 120cm/4ft long and two identical bangles.*

Preparation *Slide one of the bangles on to your arm and up your sleeve so that it is hidden (illustration 2).*

● ● ● ● ● ● ● ● ● ● ● ● ● ● ● ● ●

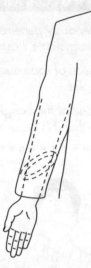

2

1 Give the rope and the second bangle to the audience so that they can be examined. Ask them to check that there are no slits, cracks or holes in the bangle – except for the hole in the middle!

Then ask someone to tie the rope around your wrists. It is important that it is tied tightly so that the audience do not think you can slip the rope over your wrists. Take the examined bangle and turn around (illustration 1).

2 With your back to the audience place the examined bangle in your breast pocket and slide the duplicate bangle down your sleeve, over your wrist and on to the rope.

3 Turn around to show that the bangle is now on the rope (illustration 3)! Once again, you can get the audience to examine the bangle now that it is dangling on the middle of the rope to make sure you have not tampered with it to get it on to the rope. Of course, unknown to them, it is a completely different bangle! You can also get them to check that the rope is still securely tied around your wrists.

4 You can have them untie the rope to release the bangle or reverse the actions to make it "escape".

Effect *A knot appears in the centre of a length of rope with a finger ring tied in it!*

Requirements *A piece of rope and a finger ring.*

Preparation *Thread the ring on to the rope. Hold the rope in your right hand with the ring concealed in your fist (illustration 1).*

● ● ● ● ● ● ● ● ● ● ● ● ● ● ● ● ●

TOP TIPS FOR TRICKSTERS

The quickest way to "fix" the ends of rope to prevent fraying is to wrap them with white or clear sticky tape. However, this is not suitable for some tricks in this book where the ends are switched for a cut piece of rope.

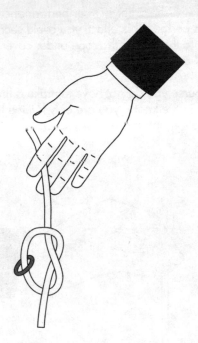

1 Perform "Another One-handed Knot" with the ring in position (illustration 2).

2 Keep the ring concealed with the back of your hand as you make the knot. It will appear tied on the centre of the rope when the knot appears (illustration 3).

To make this an even more impressive effect you could borrow a ring from a member of the audience and make it vanish earlier in your performance. When you come to perform this effect, you could secretly slide the ring on to the end of the rope under cover of your other "props" on the table.

Of course you do not have to make a finger ring appear in the knot – you are only limited by your imagination and the size of your hands!

3

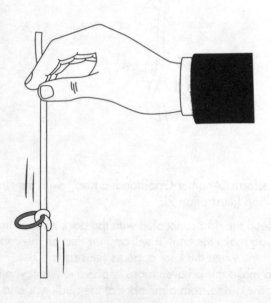

Effect A ring, securely knotted on the centre of a rope, is magically released.

Requirements A ring, a long piece of rope (about 1m/3ft) and a short piece (about 25cm/10in).

Preparation Tie a slip knot in the centre of the long rope, but do not pull the loop tight (illustration 1). Pass the short piece of rope through the ring (illustration 2). Slip the ends of the short piece of rope into the slip knot (illustration 3). The slip knot is then tightened to hide the ends of the short rope inside the knot. The extra piece appears to be a loop knotted in the rope (illustration 4).

• • • • • • • • • • • • • • • •

1

Make a slip knot
in the long piece
of rope.

Thread the short piece of rope through the ring.

Explain that you are going to demonstrate the power of magic. It doesn't matter how securely something of value is guarded – it is still possible for you to release it.

1 Display the ring knotted in the centre of the rope.

2 Ask someone to hold on to the two ends of the rope.

3 Cover the knot and the ring with a handkerchief or

TOP TIPS FOR TRICKSTERS

Rope magic is very effective because everyone is familiar with the properties of a length of rope and knows that it cannot be gimmicked or faked.

3

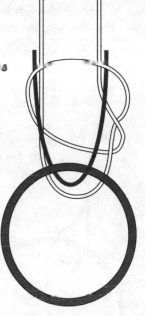

Then thread the ends of the short piece of rope through the slip knot.

TOP TIPS FOR TRICKSTERS

In all the tricks using rings or bangles it is far more effective if you are able to borrow these objects from members of the audience.

jacket. Dissolve the slip knot, releasing the short piece of rope.

4 Slip the ring off the short piece of rope and, keeping the short piece of rope hidden (under the handkerchief or jacket), show that the ring has escaped.

5 When the rope is uncovered the knot in the centre will have vanished too!

4

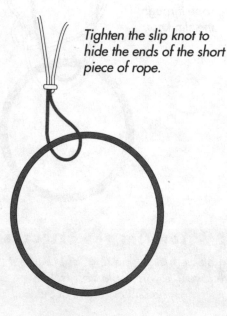

Tighten the slip knot to hide the ends of the short piece of rope.

Effect *The magician throws a borrowed bangle into a knot.*

Requirements *A length of rope and a bangle borrowed from a member of the audience.*

Preparation *None.*

● ● ● ● ● ● ● ● ● ● ● ● ● ● ● ●

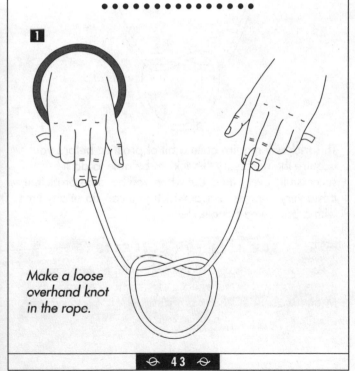

1

Make a loose overhand knot in the rope.

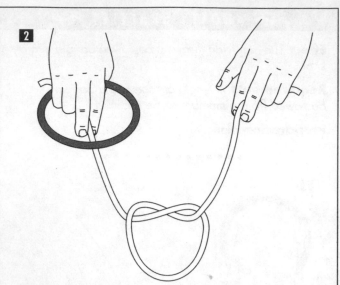

This trick will require quite a bit of practice before you acquire the necessary "knack" to be able to do it successfully every time. But when you become proficient, it is a very impressive trick which you can do at any time with a borrowed bangle.

1 Tie a loose overhand knot in the centre of the rope. Put the bangle on your right wrist. Hold the ends of the rope between the first and second fingers of each hand (illustration 1).

2 Slip the bangle over the hand on to the rope. At the same time the right thumb clips the rope to prevent the bangle from sliding down (illustration 2).

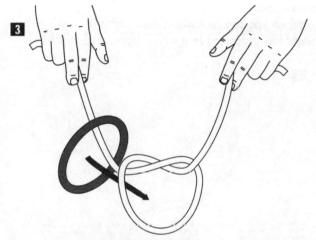

TOP TIPS FOR TRICKSTERS

To make your rope magic more visible to the audience try to hold the props at your chest level. This also encourages you to keep your head up and make eye contact with the audience.

3 The right hand throws the bangle through the loop of the knot (illustrations 3 and 4).

4 When the bangle is through, pull the knot tight. The bangle appears tied in the knot at the centre of the rope.

What actually happens is that the original overhand knot melts away and a new knot forms itself around the bangle. It is even more amazing in slow motion than it is at true speed!

When you are really confident with this trick you might feel prepared to it with a borrowed watch!

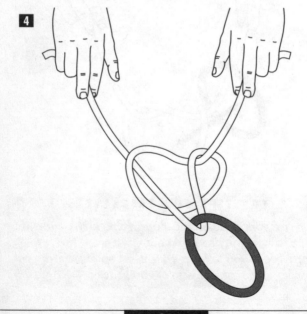

KNOTTY TRICKS

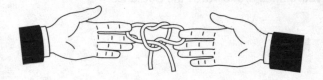

Effect *Three knots magically appear on a rope.*

Requirements *A rope about 65cm/25in long.*

Preparation *Tie a knot about 8cm/3in from each end (illustration 1).*

• • • • • • • • • • • • • • •

1 Hold the rope as in the Quick Knot with the knots concealed in your hands (illustration 1). The backs of your hands are towards the audience.

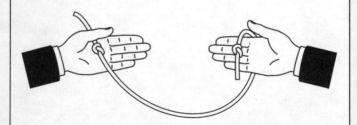

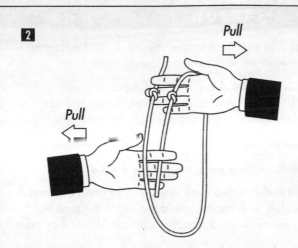

2 Perform the Quick Knot as described (illustration 2).

3 The Quick Knot will appear in the centre and the two end knots will now be seen (illustration 3).

4 All the knots seem to have appeared at the same time!

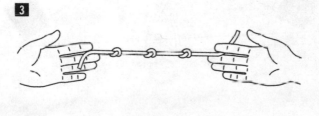

Effect *The magician throws a knot around a bangle dangling in the middle of a piece of rope.*

Requirements *A piece of stiff rope, at least 1cm/0.5in thick and about 150cm/5ft long, and a bangle (which can be borrowed).*

Preparation *Thread the bangle on to the rope.*

• • • • • • • • • • • • • • • • •

1 Hold end A of the rope in your right hand and end B in your left, with the bangle dangling in the middle. Hold your right hand about 15cm/6in higher than your left.

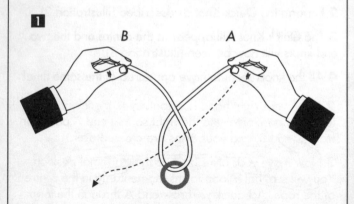

2

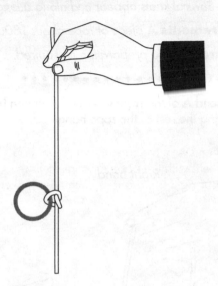

2 Move your right hand horizontally to the left and the left hand horizontally to the right so that end A passes in front of end B, and your arms are crossed over.

3 Now move your arms back to their original position. You will see that a loop forms momentarily in the centre of the rope. Act quickly. Throw end A through the loop to form a knot (illustration 1), and pull tight (illustration 2). This is a very impressive effect.

Effect *Several knots appear tied along a length of rope.*

Requirements *A piece of rope about 180cm/6ft.*

Preparation *No preparation is required.*

• • • • • • • • • • • • • • •

1 Clip end A of the rope with the left thumb (illustration 1) leaving the rest of the rope hanging free.

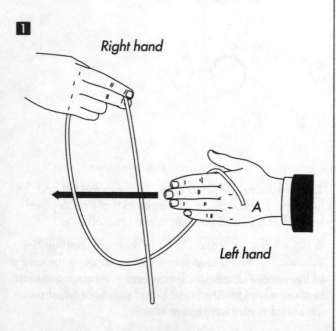

Right hand

Left hand

A

2

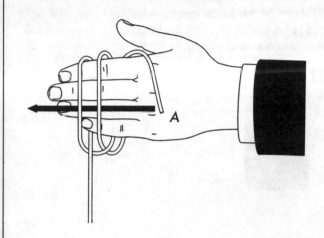

2 Take hold of the free rope at the centre with the right hand and lift it up with the first and second fingers (illustration 1). Twist the fingers away from you and hang the resulting loop on the left hand (illustrations 1 and 2).

3 Repeat step 2 to form another loop and drape this over the left fingers.

4 The number of loops you can make will depend on the length of the rope. The number of loops will equal the number of knots that appear.

5 Slip the first and second fingers of your right hand through the loops on your left hand (illustration 2) and grip end A of the rope. Pull end A through the loops and shake all the loops free from the left hand. The right hand holds end A and lets the loops drop. They will fall down the rope and magically form knots (illustration 3).

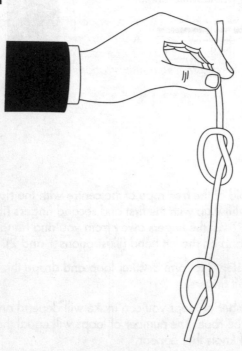

3

Effect *The audience watch the magician tie a genuine knot in a piece of rope. The magician then slides the knot along the rope and it comes off the end! The audience can keep the knot as a souvenir!*

Requirements *A long length of rope and a short piece of rope tied into a knot.*

Preparation *Place the knot in a pocket on your right side. Tie a slip knot (see page 17) in one end of the rope (we will call this end A). Hold end A in your left hand keeping the knot concealed (illustrations 1 and 2).*

● ● ● ● ● ● ● ● ● ● ● ● ● ● ● ● ●

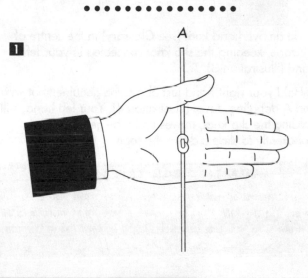

A

1

2 *The slip knot is hidden in your left hand.*

A

1 Tie an overhand knot (see Glossary) in the centre of the rope, keeping the slip knot concealed in your left hand (illustration 3).

2 Hold your right hand just above the genuine knot with end A dangling down (illustration 4). Your left hand, still holding the slip knot, moves up to the genuine knot, apparently to slide it down the rope.

TOP TIPS FOR TRICKSTERS

Remember not to use white rope when you are wearing a white shirt or jacket. If you must wear white, make sure you use coloured rope so that the audience can see the props!

3 But in fact your right hand covers the genuine knot as your left hand slides down the rope towards end A (illustration 5). Open the left hand to show the slip knot. The audience will believe this to be the genuine knot.

4 Now move the left hand and end A to the top, keeping the right hand over the genuine knot. Reverse the action in stage 3, moving the right hand up to the slip knot (taking the genuine knot with it) and apparently sliding the knot back to the centre.

3

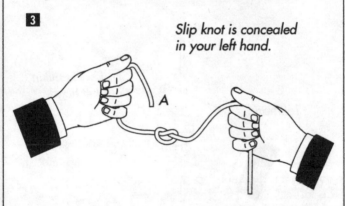

*Slip knot is concealed
in your left hand.*

A

TOP TIPS FOR TRICKSTERS

As rope is very inexpensive it is always a good idea to finish your routine by passing your piece of rope out to the audience to keep as a souvenir.

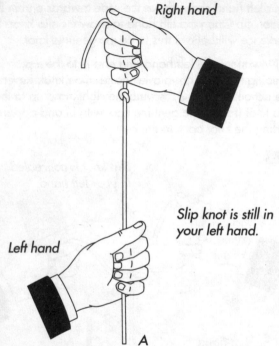

4

Right hand

Slip knot is still in your left hand.

Left hand

A

5 While the right hand covers the slip knot, tug on the rope with the left hand to "vanish" the slip knot. At the same time slide the right hand to the centre. Remove the right hand to show the knot is back where it began – in the centre.

6 You can have the rope and knot examined at this stage. While the audience are doing this, slip your right hand into your pocket and secretly take hold of the loose knot.

7 As you take back the rope, secretly slip the second and third fingers of your left hand into the loop of the genuine knot. Show the audience the knot in your hand.

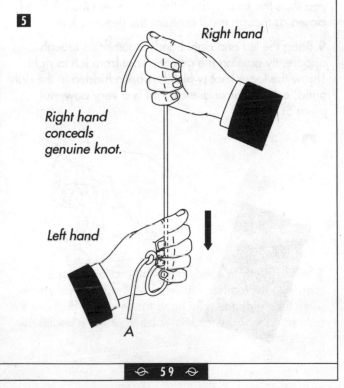

5

Right hand

Right hand
conceals
genuine knot.

Left hand

A

Close your left hand into a fist, keeping the fingers towards you to conceal the loop of rope running over them (illustration 6).

8 With the right hand hold tightly to the rope coming out of the top of the fist and slide your left hand down. The knot will slide down the rope. Continue to the end of the rope, where the knot will untie. It looks as though you slide the knot right off the rope. Keep the left hand closed as though it still contains the genuine knot.

9 Bring the left and right hands together as though apparently passing the genuine knot from left to right. Throw the loose knot (which has been hidden in the right hand) out to your audience. This is a very powerful piece of magic!

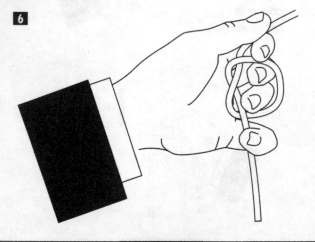

6

Effect *The magician ties a bow in a rope and pulls the ends through the bow to make a giant knot. When the audience blows on it the knot melts away.*

Requirements *A piece of soft white rope about 1m/3ft long.*

Preparation *None.*

• • • • • • • • • • • • • • • •

1 Drape the rope over your hands as shown in illustration 1. Your right hand should be behind your left and slightly higher. The palms of your hands are facing you and the backs are towards your audience.

1

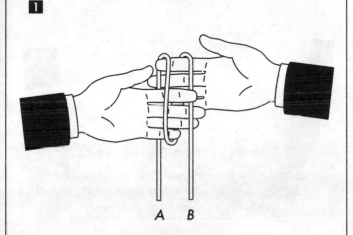

A   B

2 Clip the rope between the first and second fingers of each hand as shown in illustration 1.

3 Holding tightly to the bits of rope clipped between your fingers, move your hands slowly apart. As your hands move apart the clipped portions will form two loops of a bow (illustration 2). Continue pulling until the bow is pulled tight. You can then ask your audience if they ever get knots in their shoelaces – and explain that this is what you do if you are a magician!

4 Transfer the loops to the third finger of each hand. With the left thumb and first finger reach through the left loop and pull end A through (illustration 3).

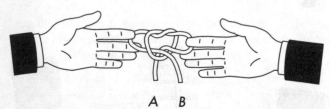

A   B

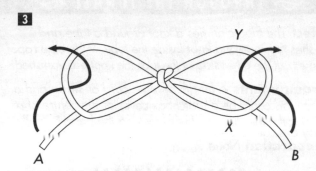

3

Y

X

A

B

5 Give the right hand loop a half twist, bringing Y forward towards you. Then with your right thumb and first finger reach through the right hand loop and pull end B through (illustration 3).

6 Pull on the two ends of the rope and the bow will get smaller, becoming what appears to be a tangled knot. In fact this is a dissolving knot all set to vanish!

7 Ask your audience to blow on the knot. As they do so, pull hard on the ends and the knot will vanish!

TOP TIPS FOR TRICKSTERS

You may think that some of the methods in this book are too simple too fool anybody. Don't worry! All the best tricks are based on simple principles.

Effect *The magician ties a knot around a tube and pushes the rope and knot inside the tube. When the rope comes out the other side of the tube the knot has vanished!*

Requirements *A length of rope, cord or string and a tube. This could be a matchbox cover or the centre of a toilet roll – the more ordinary looking the better!*

Preparation *None.*

● ● ● ● ● ● ● ● ● ● ● ● ● ● ● ●

1 Ask the audience if they have ever heard of black holes. Explain that you have one with you, and bring out your tube! You can say, "Don't laugh, this is a

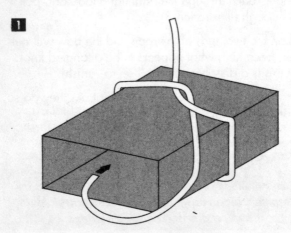

2

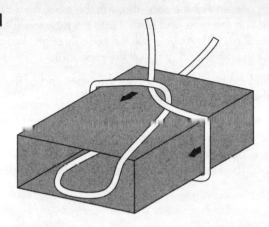

serious scientific experiment to discover what happens in black holes."

2 Drape the rope over the tube and tie a regular overhand knot around the tube (illustration 1).

3 Explain that anything can exist outside a black hole – like the knot, for example – but when things go through a black hole, anything can happen!

TOP TIPS FOR TRICKSTERS

Coloured rope is available from the haberdashery section of most department stores.

4 Push one end of the rope through the tube, then slide the knot off the tube and push it into the tube too (illustrations 2 and 3). As you pull the rope through, keep hold of the other end and pull the rope taut.

5 When the rope emerges from the other end of the tube the knot has completely vanished!

6 What really happens is this: removing the knot from around the tube forms a slip knot (illustration 3), and this comes undone inside the tube as you pull the rope through. The knot has disappeared into a black hole!

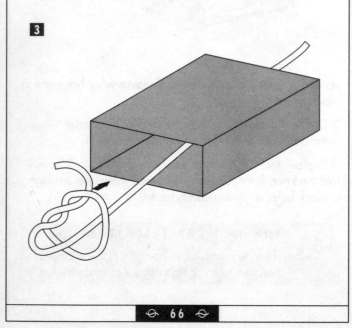

SIMPLE ESCAPES

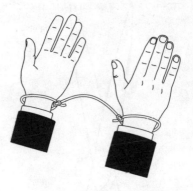

Effect *A piece of string is tied securely around the handle of a pair of scissors – yet the scissors magically escape!*

Requirements *A pair of scissors and a piece of string.*

Preparation *No preparation is needed.*

1

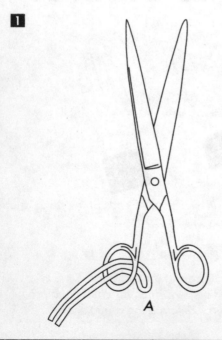

A

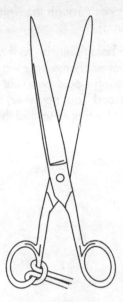

1 Double the string and thread the centre loop A through the left handle of the scissors.

2 Thread the loop A over the two ends of the string and pull tight (illustration 2).

TOP TIPS FOR TRICKSTERS

It is worth remembering that rope tricks are very versatile and can be performed for children, a group of friends or before a large audience.

3 Thread the two ends through the right handle of the scissors (illustration 3).

4 Ask someone to hold tightly on to the two ends of the string. Point out that surely the only way to release the scissors from the string would be to cut through the string with the scissors! You, however, are going to remove the scissors by magic so that the string remains undamaged.

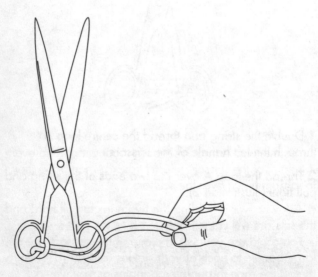

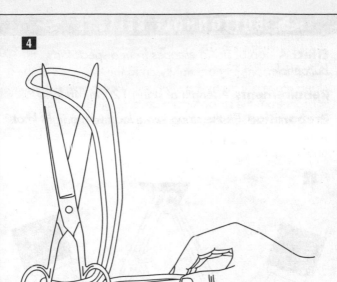

4

5 Pull the loop A through the right handle and up over the point of the scissors (illustration 4). Then bring the loop right down over the scissors.

6 Ask whoever is holding the two ends to pull hard and the scissors will come free!

You could use yourself in place of the scissors! Tie a large bangle to each of your ankles using cord. Then thread the rope through the bangles as you would through the handles of the scissors.

Effect *A loop of string escapes from a spectator's buttonhole.*

Requirements *A length of string 120cm/4ft long.*

Preparation *Tie the string into a loop with a tight knot.*

• • • • • • • • • • • • • • • • •

1

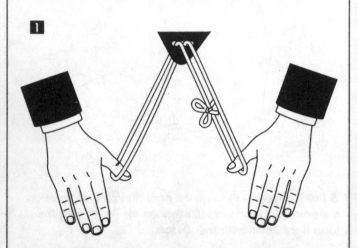

TOP TIPS FOR TRICKSTERS

Remember that white rope can get dirty very quickly when you rehearse with it. Always try to use a fresh piece of rope for each performance.

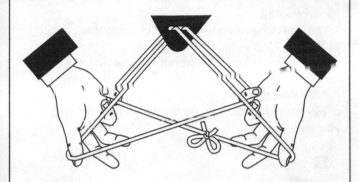

2

1 Thread the loop through the buttonhole of a spectator, and hook your thumbs through each end of the loop (illustration 1).

2 Bring your hands together. Insert the little fingers as shown in illustration 2 – each picks up the lower strand from the opposite side.

TOP TIPS FOR TRICKSTERS

When using silk handkerchiefs in your rope magic always ensure that they are ironed and pressed before each performance. Audiences DO notice.

3 Release the left little finger and the right thumb, at the same time pulling the loop tight. The loop will appear to pass through the buttonhole without damaging it (illustration 3).

You can achieve an even more exciting effect by pulling the loop of rope through your own neck! It works the same way – bring the hands together in front of the neck, engage the fingers and pull with one side as you release the other. This is a very dramatic effect because of the danger involved – be careful you don't throttle yourself!

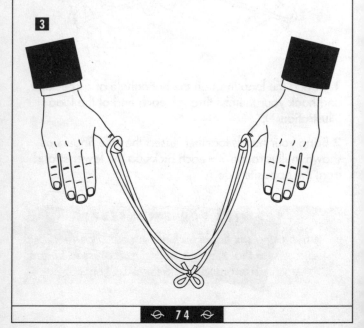

Effect *The magician and a spectator are tied securely together, but they manage to escape by magic.*

Requirements *Two ropes, each 120cm/4ft long.*

Preparation *No preparation is required.*

● ● ● ● ● ● ● ● ● ● ● ● ● ● ● ●

1 Tie one of the ropes around the wrists of the spectator (illustration 1).

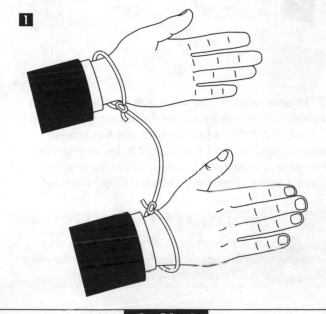

1

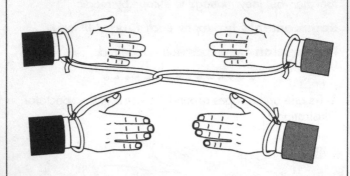

2 Have someone tie your wrists with the other rope, first
threading it through the loop of the first rope (illustration 2).
  Explain that this is how convicts are transported
around together, and it is thought to be very secure.
However, it does not take into account the magical
powers passed down to you by the Great Houdini!

TOP TIPS FOR TRICKSTERS

*Escapes are much more effective if you use the
strongest looking person in the room to tie the knots
and make sure you are secure.*

3 It seems impossible for you to escape, but it can be done. Pull the centre loop A of the spectator's rope and thread it under the loop tied around your left wrist. When you have enough rope pulled through pull it over your left hand (illustration 3).

4 If the spectator now steps back you will both be free! With practice you can learn to do step 3 in just a few seconds.

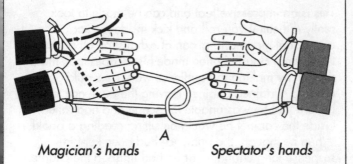

A

Magician's hands   *Spectator's hands*

TOP TIPS FOR TRICKSTERS

Your rope will stay cleaner and whiter longer if you ensure your hands and nails are kept clean before practice sessions, rehearsals and performances.

Effect *The magician escapes, like the Great Houdini, from a big canvas sack.*

Requirements *A canvas sack, big enough for you to sit in comfortably, which has eyelets around the top with a long piece of rope threaded through them. You also need a screen or cover.*

Preparation *There is no preparation.*

• • • • • • • • • • • • • • • •

This is an impressive feat and can be made to look really difficult if you roll and kick inside the sack. The occasional moan and groan of exhaustion all adds to the drama! Houdini often made his escapes look more difficult by making the audience wait. He would go inside a curtained cabinet, leaving the audience to believe that he was unable to escape and had failed. Inside the cabinet he would be sitting reading a book! When he thought the audience had been kept in suspense long enough – or he had finished the chapter! – he would stumble out of the cabinet, as though he was exhausted, free once again!

TOP TIPS FOR TRICKSTERS

If you are performing for children it is always a good idea to use coloured rope to add visual appeal.

1

*Get into the sack, keeping hold
of a long loop of rope.*

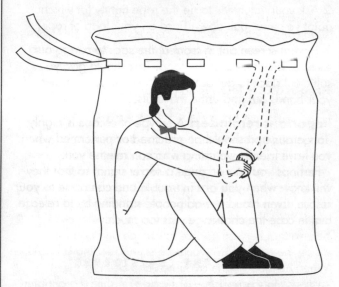

TOP TIPS FOR TRICKSTERS

*One of the main reasons for Houdini's fame was
the challenge aspect that his escapes offered. People
enjoy the tension of a challenge – remember this when
performing your escapes.*

1 Climb into the sack and ask someone to tie you into it. As you climb inside pull a loop of the rope inside with you (at least 60cm/2ft).

2 Ask your volunteer to tie the rope tightly (at which point you must pull down hard on your loop of rope).

3 Have a screen put in front of the sack to cover your escape. Then let go of the loop. This should give you sufficient slack to get out of the bag. Or you can get your hands out and untie the knots.

Important reminder: Any type of escape is highly dangerous and should be practised or performed when you have friends watching who can release you.

Perhaps you can arrange a secret signal so that they will know when you are in trouble and can come to your rescue. Even Houdini had people standing by to release him in case the challenge was too much.

MILBOURNE CHRISTOPHER

Milbourne Christopher was one of the most prominent American magicians in the second part of the twentieth century. He toured the world with his own big illusion show, appeared on Broadway and starred in some of America's first televised magic "specials", paving the way for the likes of Doug Henning and David Copperfield. But the show's highlight was a rope routine, admired by magicians the world over.